BLACKJACK-22

Modern Poetry

Robert Deshaies II

Copyright © 2020 Robert Deshaies II
All rights reserved
First Edition

Fulton Books, Inc.
Meadville, PA

Published by Fulton Books 2020

ISBN 978-1-64654-561-2 (paperback)
ISBN 978-1-64654-562-9 (digital)

Printed in the United States of America

For Joseph
and
For Mom, Dad, Simone

MY WORLD

If I had to make a world for myself, it would be simple. It would be identical to the world we live in today. Imagine if hate, greed, regret, pain, suffering, resentment, depression, anxiety, and fear disappeared. Where is the humanity in robotic creation? Where is the essence within a machine? I ask. My world exists in an amalgamation of the everyday apocalypse of a divided world and the underwhelming tiredness of lost love within a self-destructive nature. I wouldn't have it any other way, to be brutally honest. It may be intolerable at points, but if I look close enough, you can see through another lens.

We see black, white, and for some, rainbow. Do we ever blend the tones to create grays?

Love is a thing that is binding, and it is a thing of breaking as well. I wish peace and fortune on those who seek that endless love, but let me tell you it is few and far between. Some say the realism of the world is too impolite or heartbreaking, but how can love flourish without the hate in it? Does a swamp not grow life? Even with an image of decay in a person's mind, a swamp is often filled with some of the most diverse life on the planet. How about that college crush that you hated so much because of their arrogance and pride? Oh, wait, they're the one you married because you saw the potential and held on. Or how about the love born from generations of hate between cultures? Isn't forgiveness of another for apologizing for a wrong not love in its most pure essence?

I expand.

How can we hope to understand such complex ideas like love without first understanding the knowledge that there are things far above our understanding and comprehension? Love transcends all things—space, time, cultures, language, art, dance, cuisine, and if you really think about it, if hydrogen didn't love oxygen, then we wouldn't have water. Atomic love. The shared bond within all things is a universal balance, but—and this is my opinion—it is also a giant orgasm of universal truth. Yes, that sounds absolutely ridiculous, but hear me out. Sex is a ritual that almost everyone partakes in. I don't really care about the sexual aspect or the number of people it takes to classify a sexual act; I care about its essence. It's a celebration of affection, physical love, diversity, and in some ways, transcendence above just physical desire and the realization or observance of a shared union uniting a group of people. Incredible, right?

But then again, my opinion is most likely, and I'm serious, infinitesimal in comparison to the true meaning of love. I don't have it figured out; no one does. We must keep trying, though; through the pain, through the anxiety, through the insane torture of falling in love, we must keep trying. This is the world I live in, and I wouldn't have it any other way.

It's tireless, it's suicidal, it's stupid, but it's also clear as day.

Love. Undying. Eternal.

To whoever needs this, I love you and you are loved. You are incredible, unique, and capable of receiving and giving love.

Cheers!

PS: When you're there, let me know. I'll be waiting with open arms.

LOVE
Part One

You caress me as your curves rhythmically move with synchronous motion of your words. As I brush along my canvas, you bite and gnaw at my flesh. Instinctively you know what to say, and I beg for more. You tell me everything I want to hear, and I follow in accordance. I stroke and look to brush again, but you tell me to stop. I ask why, and you say, "Because this isn't love."

Desire and love are where my lines begin to blur. Am I truly in love, or am I in love with the concept?

Here I am, giving you everything that I am, but the movement is lost to me. With each passing stroke, the passion dissipates and no climax is reached. In the moments after we halt our proceedings, you light a cigarette.

Ah, that pungent smell. I look at you, and you me. I search. I search for what it was that I thought was the love we had. Or has it been a ploy this entire time? The cigarette gets shorter as your responses follow accordingly. Conversation turns to stabbing bursts, and I ask for a light.

As we both bask in the aroma, the haze seems to provide a clarity that burns just the tip of a momentous thought. I inhale and turn. She looks at me and exhales. The colliding forces ignite something that I never even thought to question before.

"If I really am in love with you, would you die for me?"
Another inhale. "I don't know…"
Exhale.

BRUTALITY

A Message as Frank As It May Be

How dare you! How fucking dare you!

    The accusation, it's defaming, it's demoralizing, it's brutal…

    Yet you stare, unfaltering. Your heart barely skipped a beat when you said it. That's how brutal you have become. Unforgiving, merciless, hateful—these are the words that I would've never fathomed you capable of producing. You see, I would never, and you know that's the frank and honest truth.

    Dear Frank, where have you been? I miss you; I miss us. The love we had, it was precious, time-consuming to the point where I didn't care how we spent it. In the moments when our hearts skipped together, joined hands and all, in a manner of brutality, you beat it to death.

    Frank.

    The beating, the punishment, and the terror you created, I resented. To be completely honest, I do not anymore. For how can I? Pretty and petty like a penny unclean and unbrushed, left on the street. You made me unwanted. You defiled it in such a lying manner that I questioned, Was it worth it?

    Well, to be frank, it goddamn was. You run scared now that you realized all you lost. In the swift, brutal seconds, you realized. An overwhelming and vicious terror ruthlessly reaps your soul. I'm sorry, I truly am. I don't know what happened, and to be frank, I hope the pain subsides. I hope the agony washes away, but I know it won't. Brutality was your only way to get out, you thought. Well, tables have been turned, and now you see that your own actions have sown your own destruction. How severely perfect.

    Frankly, I couldn't see any other result forming. Welcome to the absence, darling.

    Enjoy your stay.

    Be wary, for the steps we take in life are often judged in death.

SEARCHING

I Can't See a Horizon

I have loved and will find love again. When will it be the last? I wonder.
    When will it the be truest of true?
    I don't know, but when I do…
    No, wait, I need to continue searching. After what feels like a lifetime of love lost, I have experienced pain, loss, regret, happiness, and most importantly, the true lesson that is love.
    Love is not defined by one simple relationship or act; in fact, I have been searching my entire life to find something even close to resembling its entire essence.
    Is that possible? To be honest, I don't think I will ever know, but I guess I must keep trying. Often, I will reel in a catch who I think is the one, but heartbreak prevails.
    In the brokenness, I discover the true meaning of the search.
    Searching in an ocean that is impossibly vast, but like the fish I am, I must keep swimming. I find my flock, and I leave once I am no longer wanted, but I know my love will never fade from the ones I have touched.
    Once they have let me free, in hopeless abandonment, I continue to search for the true.
    It hurts and it hurts, but I will never give up.

    Searching in a sea too large for even me to consider the vastness.

If you take my hand now, I will show you what can come of this.
This trust in the fall, *it's a leap of faith.*
I reach out…
Our hands don't touch.
I fall.

WHY?
Guilt

Why did you do it?
    How could you? I sit here, hands in my face, and I loom up. You're still there, mocking me. Flaunting your excellence and beauty over thy own. Who are you to think that you…?
    "Oh, I'm sorry. I didn't know. It's my fault? No. Wait, you're right. It is. I'm sorry."
    The endless apology continues on and on; it's a broken record at this point. I'm saturated in your condescending voice.
    You remain. I leave. Is that not how it goes? The blame resonates inside, and I carry it without pride.

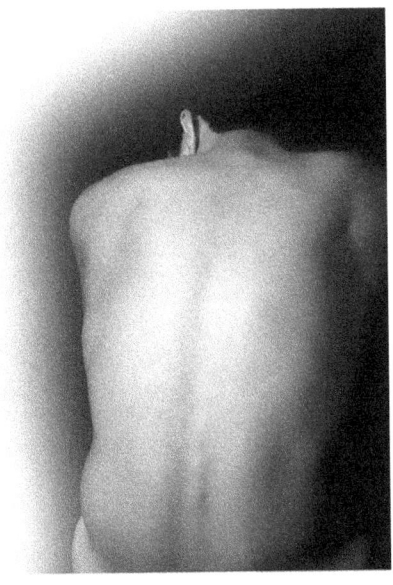

The Guilt
Joseph Deshaies

DRUNK

Intoxication

I sit here.

    I sit here with my glass.

    The glass is half-empty. Half-empty on the day of my birth. How poetic that I choose now. Now, the day I was birthed into existence, is the day I hate the most. I hate myself. *Wash it down,* my head tells me. *Take another. Another.* Is that music I hear in the background? Is someone calling for me? Or is it the liquor that stares at me, speaking?

    "Oh, darling. Yes, I know. I was supposed to call you, but...it was just that one time, right? Oh, you caught feelings...well, did you ever consider mine? Don't make this about me? Fuck you. No. I'm sorry...Hey, I'm sorry...I apologize."

    We hug.

    I offer her a drink.

HIGH

Euphoria, a.k.a. Teenage Rebellion

Ha. Ha. Ha.
"Why are you so serious, man? Why are you so strict? Why do you follow the rules? The guidelines are radical propaganda, man."
"They want you to turn to them. They want conformity, man. Absolute control over us. Totalitarian bastards."
"Oh, you want a drag?"
Inhale…exhale…
"Oh. Now, that's the spot."
Ha. Ha. Ha.
I don't know, man. Maybe the rules are stupid; maybe guidelines exist because people are more comfortable with conformity. Radicals are the face of change! Right? Aren't we supposed to question authority? Aren't we supposed to produce our own thought? You know, live our own lives outside the influences of the society. Oh, wait, man, can I grab another?
Inhale…exhale…
"Wait, do you feel that? The Earth…it's rotating. Man, that's insane."
Heh.
No, wait. It's all a joke.
Ha. Ha. Ha.

SOBER

The Obvious yet Arduous Choice

A clarity like no other, it's often boring and uneventful, painful even. As I lie in the corner, cradled, I shiver and squirm like a fly plucked of its wings, helpless. It hurts. I think I'm going to die. The pain, the shivers, the mood swings…I know I can end it, the pain.

"Take another," the infamous line is whispered into my ear, but no one lies beside me. Am I going insane? Or is it this damn cold turkey? I've never felt like this before; all my life it's been a mostly clear head, but now I can't seem to find the right road to stroll down.

There's a fork in the road now; it's time to make a choice.

My teeth chatter as I rub my arms up and down my fragile frame. Even the slightest of movements is upsetting; I can't seem to break this grasp. Why can't I choose a damn road already? Is it the lack of control that I like? Do I really need these to perk me up every damn day? Then again, it's euphoria. The feeling that I am a part of the collective. The collective of users who have swamped me my entire life.

Right or left? Goddamnit, choose! My brain is screaming, and my head pulsates. I fall. In the haze I see two figures approach. *Are they real?* I think to myself. I'm in the middle of nowhere. How can this be? As the figures approach, both reach out to lend a hand. Who do I trust? Right or left? Both figures smile, and they say, "Come on, let's go. I can give you everything you need." Their voices echo through my skull. The sound bounces and bounces from ear to ear, repeating rhythmically. Right or left? Choose, goddamnit! I gather myself; I think this is it. The end of the line. A crossroad with no destinations except right or left.

The choice is mine; it always has been. Can I make the decision? It's hard to say. All I know is the pain will end. Everything ends. At least I hope it does. I get to my feet, and I look at the two still reaching out for me. Then it hits me; no matter what I choose, I know I can be unshackled from this pain. All it takes is a choice…

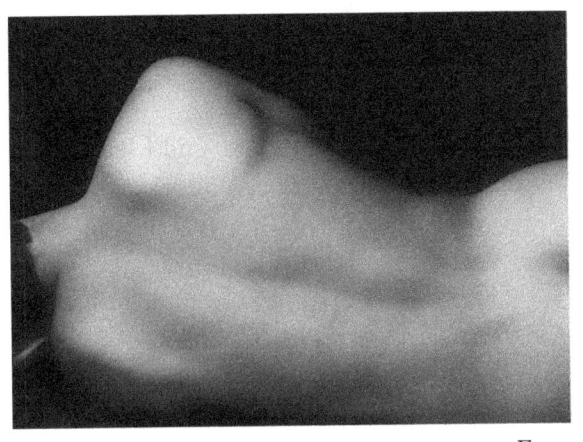

Fever
Joseph Deshaies

CROSS

The Weight of My Soul

My sins exist because of you, and I hate you for that.
You should have never been born. I *hate* you!
Now. Why now? I hate myself; I hate myself more than I hate you.
I do not wish you ill will...
I...I'm selfish. No, I agree, I shouldn't have raised my voice.
Do you ever look back?
You know, when you were young?
Everything was innocent and carefree.
Whatever happened to a world without heartbreak?
You talk like this, I talk like that...you and me.
You and I were there for it. We were there.
We took it slow. We kept it easy for...we kept to the rules.
Some semblance of order. Oh. I see. You broke the rules. Rules are for breaking, you say.
Ha. Wait. Was I begging for forgiveness when I should've been accepting it?
No. So I'm not Jesus.
Oh, honey, I know.
Time breaks my back piling onto the weight of your love.
It's gone. I no longer have to deal with it. I can do whatever I want.
I can drink...
I can smoke...
I can do...heh.
A burden, can't you see?
This is what I carry.

HATE

The Hard Truth

Which is strongest? Hate or love?
    Because all I see is hate. In every image, in every flutter of color stabbing my eye, I see a barrage of hate. It just piles onto one another like maggots slithering from a decomposing corpse. *I hate you.* Three simple words that have brought conflict since the beginning of man.
    When we disagree in beliefs, cultures, language, and for God's sake, even the goddamn place to eat for dinner, we feed this infection as if we simply want our lives to be bound to the coffin in the ground already.
    Resentment leads to hate. Evil mirrors it. Yet hate is the rawest, most unrelenting, and most powerful emotion in the universe. It's so potent that its polar, love, is unrelenting as well to ward off the contagion that is hate. *But*—and I sincerely believe in this—without hate, where would we be?
    Without hate and ignorance, would we never fully realize that our vision was blinded? Would we never have the blessing to comprehend that love, compassion, and hope can conquer even the strongest of fears, hate, and avarice? Hate is conquering; I do not deny this. Yes, it can be apocalyptically overwhelming, but you *hate* that, don't you?
    You hate that you can't just preach one side as opposed to the other? You want to be able to preach and propagate just one mission.
    Upsetting the balance.
    That…and that is unforgivably hateful of you.
    Acceptance and understanding. Understand what it is you hate before classifying it ignorantly. Understand me; I try to love you, but at some point, I will pour pure, unrelenting hate into you because I am human. I lose control and become upset.
    All I ask is that you understand before labeling so quickly.
    All I ask is for an "I love you" before an "I hate you."

RELIGION
My Eternal Struggle

I have often wondered why the religious are often the most hypocritical.
　Dogma, rituals, and endless preaching.
　My god, I cannot get enough of the bullshit that falls from their mouths.
　"You need to *do this* to earn your salvation"
　Another teaching states, "Turn the other cheek always, otherwise you will be cursed to hell, and such."
　Religion is the longest lie in the entirety of existence.
　Wars, bloodsheds, massacres, persecutions, inquisitions.
　You name it, it's all been ordered by a hierarchy who has more "faith" than you and I.
　I am not an atheist, but I am also not religious.
　Yes, I have faith, but it is faith in humanity.
　Not some false god promising me all will be better, "in the end."
　How can I wait for a savior to come when I can do saving of my own?
　I am not a prophet, nor am I a priest. I do not preach or tell you to follow my beliefs. I simply ask that you listen, and through listening you begin to understand.
　We aren't perfect—far from it, in fact. There is a common lie across most beliefs, the idea that we can be perfected by following a certain path.
　You and I do not walk the same path. We share experiences, pains, loves, etcetera.
　The foundation upon which a religion is born flows from a singular truth bred for the masses to hear. Its name is [redacted]. Once the masses hear this invisible calling of the ultimate truth, a religion is born.
　A foundation born. Oddly specific dogma instilled. My struggle.

How can you tell me to act and be because I was supposedly born from something divine? I am not immortal, divine, or something eternal. I am human. I do not know where I will go when I die, but actions, good and evil, have consequences. If it's a hell of my own making, then so be it. I will strive to be good, but I know I will falter.

Share your beliefs, but do not preach them to me.

Conversion is a sin.

You betray everything you could ever become by listening to the lie.

ANGER

The Worst Parts of Me

I'm angry.

I'm angry all the time, it seems.

It's hard to remember a time when I wasn't angry.

It's right there below the surface, dwelling, waiting to be unleashed.

The anger subsides momentarily, but at times the monster needs to be set free.

It's a reckoning that I wish upon no one, but it is uncontrollable at points.

Words, the flame that fuels the unforgiving fire of my disturbed peace.

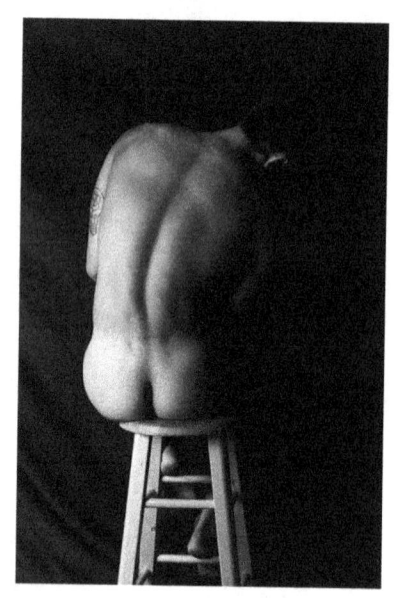

Hiding from Myself
Joseph Deshaies

WHAT IS A FRIEND?
F.R.I.E.N.D

Forever you will be…
Rendered psyches correlate.
Infinitely optimal compatibility success.
Empathetically diverse and rich.
Neither selfish nor selfless, but perfectly placed in the middle.
Detailed analysis complete—would you like to confirm your match?
I need you, but I won't be your forever.
We are similar, yes, but we do not agree on everything.
Across time and space, you have remained there; albeit, it in the grand scheme that's quite insignificant.
Our emotions resonate with one another because we have experienced the same pain and we both haven't grown from it yet.
"I'm sorry, it's just that…well, you know. Yes, this is important for *me*!"
Aristotle once said, "A friend is a single soul dwelling in two bodies," but I find that quite baffling, don't you?
I am me. You are you.
So what are we?
Confirm?
Maybe.

FATALE

Femme

Her glance bites me, a snake wandering the unknown field.
Her touch breaks my precious mind, glass shatters, and my subconscious breaks.
Her kiss plants itself to me; poison secretes into my soul.
She is fatal, and yet I can't stop thinking about her.
The touch and kiss of death that springs me to life.
Is she the one trying to rescue me? Or I her?
We halt our long walk as she grasps my hand for the last time, and she speaks…
"I'm sorry, but I don't want to hurt you anymore."
I can't piece a sentence together, because I know it has been a ticking clock.
The midnight hour approaches, and it's time to leave.
She kisses me farewell, and with her final touch, a piece of her is planted.
Planted so deep in my memory that I will never forget.
The memory of the woman who not only saved my soul but also destroyed my spirit.

HEAVEN

The Fleeting Dream

Grace. We are all born with it. Yet we are far from perfect. But how can our perception of perfection continue to exist in such a degrading world? The loss of control in our upbringing, does it lead to this? The image painted in our head. You know, the one our mother depicted to us as a child. The perfect place. The silver city. The shining star. It's the ultimate lie. Is that truly all we have to look forward to? An eternity in a perfect world? How *boring*!

 Cough. Oh, I don't feel so well. *Cough. Cough.* That's not a good sign.

 Cough. Cough. Cough. I stagger, my feet falling from under me.

 Crack. Hello? I need help. Please. Senses are going numb. I don't know what's going on. Fuck. It's really dark in here. No, wait, is that a light? Hello? Hello! I trip forward and hit my head.

 Fuck. Oh. Oh. Wow, this place is beautiful. It's everything I could imagine. I'm in love. No. I'm wrong. Oh, this is a place that is meant to be shared. So like anybody? No way. That's amazing. My last name? Yes, oh yes, it's...what? I'm not allowed in? Oh. I see, it's a race thing, right? I'm not allowed in because, oh. Not that? It's because it's not my time? You're sending me back? I'm needed? No, that can't be right. When has anybody ever needed me?

 A voice shutters the halls of this glistening white room. As I look up, a voice thunders into my soul.

 My thoughts disperse as one sentence protrudes and claws itself into my psyche. It tells me.

 I wake.

 Wait, was that a dream?

PAIN

The Scars Inside

I'm terrified.
 I cannot stress this enough, because I don't know what to make of this.
 This mistake. This *damn* mistake. The mistake that we could've been when we shouldn't have.
 It's a terror that I am friendly with, to my misfortune.
 The pain that rippled from the hole in my heart. The heart that was then ripped wholly from my chest, and I wasn't quick enough to realize that you played me the entire time. The mistake that causes the fear, self-questioning, anxieties, but worst of all.
 It's the equation to my pain.
 It was everything and nothing, simultaneously. I was you, and you weren't me. The miscommunication.
 You made it hard not to fall in love with you. You had it all—the hair, the eyes, the emotions, and the connection, most of all. Or was it? No, I can't think like that.
 It could've been, but it never was.
 I expected a garden when you only grew a flower.
 My pain isn't because I'm terrified of the mistakes we made; it's the pain in knowing that you threw it all away on a whim. The blinding journey into self-destruction. I followed like a lamb, yet I was thinking it was my salvation.
 Pain—a single-syllable word that's description is far beyond that. Pain is a lesson, and we are its teacher. We expose our souls and allow ourselves to experience pain because we then know how to heal.
 The pain we cradle can be the seed that grows the garden.
 I never made a mistake. Neither did you. It was us. We both did. The pain I suffered from is because we failed to realize that we

needed to express ourselves fully without the misguided wordplay between the messages we were signaling.

I am pain.

I am pain up until I get back up. Until I get back into the thick of it.

Press, expose, and dig into the scab. Expose the true meaning of my pain, but most of all, never forget. Pain is a memory worth keeping.

ROSE

Bloody Hands

It has been a while, I must agree;
The promise made so long ago was one not forgotten easily.
I remember gifting you with something that I thought precious.
The gift was a rose, the symbol of what we were and could be.
Water it, douse it in sunshine, and it will last.
No, you let it wither—*decompose, decay, die.*
You never even wrote…
You hid my flower from what it needed most: attention.
The rose that was meant to be a garden for so many more.
Forgotten, abandoned, vulnerable.
I gave you this knowing not what would come; I only prayed for the hope of what might've.
Next time I gift you a rose, just know I will not expect it to grow.
Instead, I will use its thorn to prick my thumb.
So that you may see that I can bleed.
Bleed just the same as you.

DEATH

I'm a Nihilist

Everything dies. There is no stopping this, so knowing this, how do we move forward?

The culmination of our lives ending in a single moment—quite ironic, if you ask me. It's a struggle that I see all too often, the ending. The horror of the ending, knowing there is nothing left for us after. So do we let the fear rule and run its course while we stand by already a ghost floating without intention?

I struggle, so much so that I beckon, and I call out. No one answers. Are we born to be without? Without a compass to guide us. Death seems to be the only assurance in this world at times; the destruction and pain cycling constantly is a godsent awful feeling that makes me want to choke the earth until we are all dead. Then there would be no more pain. Ending it all, finalizing what it was always meant to be.

Absolute nothingness.

That's the struggle, and I hope to overcome it. The damnation plays as we fight alongside it, denying the truth. But what is the truth at this point? Is it that everything dies? Or is it knowing that everything dies and because of that we choose to live? My grip loosens, and a fervor rekindles. I know it's coming, but I don't know when. Uncertainty flashes before my eyes, yet I remain steadfast. I fasten for the ride, and I take the wheel. After all, why let death take control? I drive.

Death is an ending, yes, but I see the beauty inside the inevitable. It's a hard lens to stare through, but in choosing to accept this fact, I have been stricken with a knowledge that is wonderful and unwavering. In this knowledge, I freely choose to accept death and live as if every day is my last. After all, we never know when it will finally unveil its ugly head and encroach.

Bless be me, for I am a soldier fighting an unwinnable war. The intrigue is in knowing that I am sacrificing nothing because I know that I will have everything in the end.

The life I imagined and lived to the fullest.

FOR THE MAN WHO HAS EVERYTHING

You lecture, I listen. You judge, I accept. You brag, I applaud.
   I teach, you deny. I humble and catch, you throw and toss.
   There isn't much difference between you and me. You think in such a way that I question, and I ponder. Is this your version of the truth? If so, then when did you become so blind?
   I lend when you steal. I help when you run. There's a difference I spot, yet you hold yourself higher.
   Why is that?
   Do you think yourself that much better?
   Tell me, have you ever considered others? Negation with a head nod.
   You hit; I turn the other cheek.
   "How dare you!" you say, and I say, "I do."
   How long till you realize that for the man who has everything, you have absolutely nothing.
   When was the last time you felt anything? When was the last time you opened yourself up to this beautiful creation we exist in? I ask this because I care. I really do.
   From the man who had lost everything and became nothing, I made something. I opened, I talked, I accepted, and most of all, I learned. Ignorance is bliss only when you are blind. You hate me now, but I will never hate you. Instead, I will try to place my right foot forward and offer my hand. I do not want to leave, even when you wander farther. I try to help this seemingly lost cause because I can see the floor cracking under your "mighty" wrath. I understand the hesitation.
   It's a mountain. Believe me, I know.
   Just know I'm here. No matter what, no matter when. I will continue to hope, to provide, to feel, and I hope you will uncover your eyes so that the magnificent truth may breach them with an

unbridled light. I do not seek to fail, but where you have, I will heal. I offer guidance, without judgment. I do not know it all, but it's a journey that I hope to walk alongside with you. After all, that blinding light, it's too glorious not to experience together. Shallow, this is not. Truth is deep, profound, and it's there. I see the glimmer deep in those eyes of yours. Beautiful in their isolation, but when the light breaks through, you can't possibly imagine what you will see.

You can become better, as can I. So for the man who has everything and nothing, why don't we expand to establish more than just a something?

A TIMELY INTERLUDE
The Uptake

Sunflowers in The Breach
Dawnmarie Deshaies

LOVE
Part Two

"*I love you.*"
No…that isn't it.
I'm not in love.
I know what love is, but…
What is love?
How can *my* love be unique in the existence of all other love?
But that doesn't matter.
I am getting ahead of myself now.
I haven't figured it out, but I will.

POLKA DOTS

Captured

I am enthralled in your gaze.
Your voice bellows through this room, and every eye is locked onto you.
Every eye is looking at you and your polka dots.
You have me caught, and your glance matches mine.
Albeit for a fleeting moment, but I receive a wink and I can't help but blush.
As my red cheeks blush further, a grin creeps its way across my face, and I begin clapping.
Your audience follows in tail, and your sound generates a perfect flurry of hand movements and body curvature.
Thoughts race through my head, and I'm sorry, but I must ask,
Are you taken?
Because you have already taken me, and it would be a terrible disaster if you were.
I continue to be amazed by the spectacle unfolding in front of my eyes, and once again we meet.
This time you walk through the crowd, your polka dot dress gliding along the floor.
As you approach, you voice becomes softer, but your character remains steady.
Arrival is here, and you turn your back toward me.
You finish the song, and the crowd gifts you with a standing ovation.
You take a seat at my table, and you turn to me from over your shoulder.
Any requests?
My face quirks into a laughing smile, and I speak.
Hey, baby, will you be my girl?

ETERNAL

How Long Is Forever?

What is eternal?
Is it forever?
Or is there a limit? A limit to what is conceived and what is created?
A strong sense that we are pulling to the impossible.
At the end of the impossible is the eternal.
The clock strikes, but it doesn't move.
"How can this be?"
Time passes, yet we remain. Not as ghosts, but as memories.
Call it whatever you like, but I hope to understand it one day.
Eternity: a concept inconceivable, yet it will continue to exist, unbroken and unwavering, forever.

INSANITY
Avant-Garde

In my opinion, every artist is insane. I am insane.

I am insane because I choose to overstep the boundaries that society has placed around *me*.

I have chosen to break those shackles and have been labeled a criminal, a delinquent, and *deviant*.

Yet I never become any such label. How can you label me insane when I have done *nothing wrong*?

I'm simply avant-garde.

Picasso was an artist; he was insane.

Fitzgerald was an artist; he was insane.

Pollock was an artist; don't even get me started on him.

Da Vinci was an artist; he was most definitely insane.

The equation to insanity? You. You're the damn answer.

A sane mind is nothing but a stale piece of bread left out too long.

What artist have you ever heard of that hasn't been surrounded by impossible *imagination*, thoughts, ideas, and words? None, absolutely none. All of them, you included, are *insane* in your own ways.

You have an expiration, so in the time you have, and the time I have, why not break some rules?

Question the authority that judges us.

This might sound crazy, but why don't we all turn insane and see how much of a legacy we can create?

HOPE

It's What Keeps Me Alive

It is precious, the little light that dwells inside. I'm immune to the flame blowing away because I hope. I hope for a better world. Peace in our time and such. It's hard to conceptualize with the immense amount of terror, destruction, and hate that erodes my soul. Yet I never waver.

From an early age, I have hoped for a future blessed with the bright fire of an eternity of peace, but I know that hope is but a dream.

Promethean: I want to understand that the fire gifted can also be taken away. In that taking, I hope that we can believe that we can reclaim. I dream and dream and dream, but the hope of it becoming true never seems to materialize.

It's hard to forget I have so much hope inside, because I keep myself exposed. I open and rarely close the doors of my life.

I express and share, yet people run. I don't know why; I speak truth.

Well, my truth, which often is just my own.

I hope you can understand where I'm coming from.

I do not wish to criticize, to undermine, to blaspheme.

I hope that you can understand and see that all truths are messages. Messages collected in an infinite number of bottles.

We hope that not all truths are correct, but in the finite time we have, understanding and appreciation for as many as we can listen to—that is the goal.

To prevent these truths—*all truths*—from surfacing is undoubtably having a sense of false hope. In that, I cannot defend.

Hope is immeasurable in quantity but in quality is finite. Cherish it, hold it, and never let it go. It will help you even in the darkest of hours.

JOY
All of You (You Know Who You Are)

As I stare and look at you, all I can fathom is how lucky I am.

How lucky am I that I have been blessed with people in my life, persons like you?

A family not born from blood but from a bond formed. A bond forged with an immense amount of happiness that I'm proud enough to bear its mark on my heart.

A mark that has its quirks, yes. But not every mark is perfect.

The thought of you rains down on me with eternal sunshine, and I pray that I never lose sight of it. I know in those wavering moments it will be hard to comprehend how I felt so lucky in the beginning even after all we have been through, but I know I'll just need to look back.

I will need to look back and see, see that smile creeping across your face. The one formed after we hugged for the first time.

The other formed in those shared moments of laughter.

The day we lost something but realized you were there next to me with open arms.

All those times, innumerable, but also unforgettable.

The joy you have brought to my life.

All I can say is thank you. Thank you for being who you are, and I hope that I repay you in kind.

The happiness formed from our bond is a remedy for the most malicious of catastrophes, and I can't say it enough how much of a pleasure it has been for me to call you *brothers and sisters.*

PARADISE

In the End

Peace.

Peace at last. How long I have hoped for it.

The beauty, the grace, the perfection, the unobservable form…

A collection of masterpieces composed into a myriad of ageless work.

I am one, and we are one.

In the split second it takes for me to realize what I have become, an eon has passed, for I have seen not only the beginning but also the end.

A form unrecognizable to most, yet it is the most well-known.

The melody in your head that vibrates through to your core, that is it.

We are just atoms and vibrations moving through space, but the music we create in harmony is some of most beautiful ever created.

Is it eight billion? Nine billion? Ten billion? We may never know. But where I am? Where I am is eternal. We are waiting; please come join.

Peace.

Peace at last. How long it has been waiting for me to enter its welcoming arms with warmth and a touch like my mother.

As my mind dissipates in the collective, my mind flashes with images of the accomplishments, the love, the hope, the quintessential collection of the beauty that is my life.

Forged in milliseconds.

Unfathomable until you're there.

Nirvana.

AWE

Sunflowers

Neurons fire and my eyes slowly awaken to the raw light peering through my shades.

A smirk creeps across my face as I can't help but admire the beauty of a sunrise.

My fingers reach up and twiddle with the black covers. They creep and slightly pull so that the light may pass through more.

I yawn, and my body tries to sink itself back into the sheets, but no, I cannot. Not now.

I will only ever be able to experience this particular miracle once.

It needs to be observed, carefully and intently. I only have minutes to analyze and admire.

Clouds scatter, shadows disperse, light appears. Intense. Pure. Warm. The light brigade attacks my pupils like a supernova exploding in the cosmos, but I can't help but adore the beauty of the sight.

How can one turn away from such a divine creation? The light scatters once more, and it's a new day. Fully, I wake. *Sniff.* Dandelion? No, it's...ah, yes. Bursting in tangerine and crisp shades of yellow, I pick the beautiful sunflower from its collective. I place it in my palm as I glance at the petite beauty.

Awesome.

OLD SOUL

Reincarnation

I wonder if I have lived a thousand lives before this.
    Was I ever a soldier, a politician, a husband, a sacrifice?
    My dreams scatter every night before I wake, and they are filled with visions of things that might've been.
    I wake knowing that my soul may have existed across an ocean of time and space, and my subconscious mind has been locked away, like a crypt forever meant to be untouched.
    Then, I truly think, I question, and I ponder.
    I peek back behind the hidden layers of my consciousness and attempt to recollect those "dreams."
    Then, I see something brighter.
    I see that I have been fortunate.
    Blessed by this old soul that I carry inside.
    I am not a hollow shell of a man; in fact, I find myself thinking about the times and places that I have been.
    Wandering through a desert, searching for a cause.
    Fighting an epic battle, remembering neither the reason nor the side. Writing a book in some old café, fantasizing about some ancient magnificence.
    How many times?
    I don't know.
    All I know is that I'm here. I live now.
    So why bask in my old soul when I can create something never lived before?
    A new life.

FEAR

The Times You Don't Know...Until Now

I have tried to kill myself more times than you know.
    Whether it be a blade, pills, a gun, or a car accident. I have thought of it all. My biggest fear?
    The fear of disappointment.
    The fear that I was nothing. I was a useless sack of meat poisoning the parlor floor with my existence.
    Broken. Spoiled. Forgotten. Afraid.
    As the monsters and demons continued to creep into my thoughts, I let them take hold. I imagined life would be easier if they would simply go away. But how could they? They are a part of me, and I them.
    "I am nothing." Infamous words that play to the familiar tune of terror. I listened and I danced to the rhythm. It was time to end it, all the times you didn't know about.
    A blade in hand, cold steel pressed against my pulsing throat. How easy it would've been.
    A bottle of pills stating the "recommended" dosage. How about a few more?
    A car pointed at the edge of a cliff; just throttle the gas a slight amount, and in an instant...
    In those moments, I discovered that my fears were never the monster, and neither was I.
    As I sat there and pondered on those occasions, the one thought that kept running through my head was this.
    All the times that I would read it and see it, I never understood until then. Fear taught me that forever it would be a part of me, but most importantly, *it taught me to be brave.*

When faced with the utter terror of self-destruction, I found that it wasn't my hesitation that prevented me from ending it, but it was something that I hadn't realized before. We fall so that we may learn to get back up. We let the fear take hold so that we can allow ourselves to become strong. Even the simple thought is arousing to me. In that arousing moment, I found only nothingness. The absence of fear, the absence of hope, and well, the absence of me.

So in those most private moments, I realized that for me to understand what fear was and who I am, I needed to be brave. I needed to look myself square in the mind and say, "I accept you." And in that acceptance, I learned to be unafraid. For the indominable will broke the shackles, and I understood.

No fear.

PYRAMIDS

A Man Named Ocean

I was listening to a man named Ocean once.
    He graced my ears with melodies of melancholy, and the hope stroked across my mind.
    That someday, I can be happy.
    Today is not that day, for I haven't reached the top of this pyramid yet.
    Lost in a desert, I find myself wandering. Is that water I see?
    No, it's an endless horizon. I begin to lose my *self-control* as my vision turns to *Pink + White*.
    I can't stop wandering, because without you I would fall into an abyss.
    Numb, I experience a warm rush flushing inside of me. *Novacane*.
    It presses me onward, but I lack the sight to see where I'm going. So, I swing the keys in my hand, and I press the ignition. My *White Ferrari* fires up like a muddled memory.
    She sounds familiar. *Godspeed*, I think. *Godspeed*.
    Can I live through this?
    Solo, I drive through fields—no, wait, near Oceans. Sorry, it's all a mess right now.
    As the warm numbness fades, I awaken to a biting feeling. My gut tenses like paint thinner plastering itself on me. Poison *Ivy*.
    I look through a *Lens* that is widening by the second. Lights flash by as my Provider calls through the car. I answer. Murmurs of some *Super Rich Kids* throwing a party in the hills.
    Perfect. Load myself up even more. The pyramid grows taller with each passing minute. Am I only prolonging the inevitable? Can I no longer pilot this plane to the ground? I'm sure as shit no *Pilot Jones*.

Success! I have arrived at this *Crack Rock*, Godspeed. I bend down to lace up my fresh *Nikes*, but I seem to lose my balance. I stagger, and a hand motions to catch me. I reach. As her hand touches mine, I feel a familiarity with her touch. I do not know her, but I want to. My faith in the old wavers, like a *Bad Religion*.

She asks if I'm okay. As my eyes lift from a sunken state to the glow of her *Pink Matter* exploding with beauty, I am unafraid. The top becomes closer. It's not as much a *Sierra Leone* anymore as it is my heart; it feels closer than it has in weeks. She tells me her name.

HERO
How to Be a "Super" Man

We aren't the greatest. We fail, and at times we allow jealousy and selfishness to rule the decision when faced with becoming that ultimate hero. It hurts when we think about it, but we brush it off. After all, how could I be the hero? Yes, I have sacrificed for the ones I love, but what about all the other people coexisting with me? Do I have the same concern, love, and hope for these people? Or is it for the ideal?

As the dictionary states, "[a hero is] a person who is admired or idealized for courage, outstanding achievements, or noble qualities," so since this is the definite definition, then how come we aren't all heroes? Am I not courageous? Have I never been awarded achievements? Have I never been told, "A job well done, ol' sport"? Heh, I just realized it...

I'm scared.

I'm scared because what if I am the hero who fails?

At times I fly higher than any superman; at others I sink to the depths, chained and broken.

I've learned. I have seen that even in the everyday failures.

Sometimes it's okay to help yourself before you help others.

We can't always be the invincible knight always confronting the clutches of the infinite black. Those forgotten achievements.

Insignificant in their moments until we look back.

It's okay.

We lose sight of what "made" us want to be a hero in the first place. All that matter is that we take that unrelenting punch and we push back. We stare into the face of the everyday hurt and pain, and we tell it.

"Guess what? I'm the hero of my story."

VILLAIN

The Fragile Line

I won.

I finally won.

I have beaten my enemy that has beaten me down time and again.

I have won, finally.

My war is not over yet. As I look up to the cracked sky, my eyes turn red and my blood flows through me like thick magma.

I freeze. I listen. Ah, there it is. The most beautiful sound in the world, but it's not just a sound. It's a sound of shrieking. It's terror. *My favorite.*

As I look down upon the bodies scattered in front of me, I see a blazoned line forged across the hallowed ground. It is leading to my throne. The capitol from which I shall build with the bodies of my enemies! *No...wait*!

This can't be right.

Why does this all feel like a bad dream?

I thought...I thought I was the hero of my story.

Knock. Knock. Knock.

I wake. I turn. I *see him*. He stands over me. Gun taut and pointed directly at you know who.

It's my time, you see. I can die knowing that I'm still the—

Bang.

All it takes is that one slipup and it crucifies you for a lifetime of doing the "good" work.

A villain's motto.

MOTHER

Reflections in the Sand

Intently, you watched as I grew into the man I have become today. It was not without reprimanding, but of those times, you made it a lesson. You taught me to care for those who would be left behind, to understand before I judged, to protect the ones I called family, even when you didn't have one to model from. The pain you held for years, the insecurities, the internal torture that ravaged and created the phantoms that withered you down never destroyed your spirit. The spirit that raised us to become. The spirit that was unbreakable, unyielding, yet loving in a degree that I could never fathom.

I couldn't be prouder to label you as my mother—the title that not every woman should bear, but I hope they will. It is an occupation designed to break, to wither, to drive insane the average person, but…

You are no average person. In dealing with internal struggles and pain, you raised me to understand and believe that the world, no matter how dark it got on some nights, was a blessing to live in. To understand the subtle beauties in the noise the waves create when crashing on the shore, to admire the painters creating whatever work of art came to their head, and the rain making music as it fell on the street. The artistic wave that helped transform you and me to uphold the human creativity and imagination was something you and I shared and will forever treasure. You grew up as much as I did, and yet you never placed yourself before me. You cradled, held, protected, and walked alongside me as my best friend and mother. A woman so strong it was frightening to most men, a woman who stared down the face of death and hatred and taught it to love. Taught these insurmountable forces to be accepting, to show compassion, and to leave something behind that one will forever be remembered by.

I cannot say this enough, but because of you who raised me to be, I will forever be eternally grateful that I was given the chance to be born to you. Because without you, I would have no one to search for and be lucky enough to be the mother of my children.

Mother's Touch
Dawnmarie Deshaies

FATHER, A WISE MAN

Prideful, yes. Strong, absolutely. Caring, no one would have ever surmised. The father that raised me was a giant among men. A hulking mass that had the most tender touch. A man with the power to influence, create, and mold worlds with his hands and voice, yet he never forgot where he came from.

Power never settled, and as much as it did drive him, he never let it consume him. He remembered his origins, for no matter how broken they were, he knew he could form a life of his own. A life that was meant to be shared, shared with the family he always wanted.

Once he achieved those goals, he refused to settle. For nothing was appetizing enough for him. He wanted the world, but not for himself. A world that was meant to be shared with the family he created. How powerful must it be for a man to lower himself under his peers and give them all he has earned! Yet he never asks for anything in return.

The pleasure and pride derived from his growth and care is infinite, and I cannot possibly fathom as to where he learned to forgive, to grow, to accept, and to love. He never once let anyone control or persuade him, for he made his own decisions. Decisions that bettered himself and his family, something that will never be forgotten to the legacy he leaves behind.

I stand here, today, and I wonder.

I wonder, Will I ever live up to this legacy? This immense amount of hope and pride that he bears on his shoulders. I look up, and I see that the sky is blue, the sun shines, and he approaches.

I consider the possibilities that I had failed time and again, yet he remained by my side and picked me up. In those broken moments, he put each piece back with the utmost care. He made me whole time and again. Each time I fell under the pressure, he never once questioned that I was not his own blood. For he taught me to be strong, he taught me to protect, and most importantly, he taught me to listen.

Admiration, love, acceptance, and compassion—the man I'm proud enough to call my *father*.

Gentle Hands
Dawnmarie Deshaies

HOW DOES IT GO?
The Reminder

Does the saying go, "You can't live until you die" or "You can't die until you lived"?
I thought by now that I've had it all figured out.
I turns out I was wrong.
The times I have almost died, yeah, they have sucked.
The edge of the abyss, falling into the ends of nothingness.
Hell, I could've died...
But I didn't.
I take my lighter, and I smoke a joint.
I sit on the sidewalk and instead of placing my head downward, I inhale and look up.
The moon shines, and it seems to be full.
I take another inhale, and I feel a touch on my shoulder.
She looks down upon me with a graceful face, and she says, "Come on, let's go inside."
I take another, throw whatever's left on the ground, and I get up.
Sometimes it's as simple as that.
Get up, go inside, be with the ones you love.
After all, you haven't lived until you've experienced living.

HARMONY

Dancing in the Stars

Music plays: the concord is mellow.
    A tune strikes while the rhythm quickens.
    I've never experienced this before, harmony.
    The tune that continues, and on, and on, like cascading waves on a beach.
    The moonlight hovers over the sound, and the natural tunes produced are so delightful that I stop.
    Halted, I look, I listen, I absorb.
    It's synchronous, it's harmonic, it's jazzed.
    Hips sway, head bobs, hands dance, and feet shake—an ensemble that has been waiting for too long to come together.
    I hope to live in this forever. A world without music or sound is barren, but I choose to become one with the harmony of it all. A collection of emotion and rhythm that is blissful, eternal, and well.
    Harmonious.

Blooming
Dawnmarie Deshaies

VIOLENCE
How I Have Become a Peaceful Man

To cast out a man's life is the most unforgiveable transgression in the wicked history of humanity. To end everything that ever was or ever could be is an infringement unto one's life that will never be forgivable to most. Violence has led to an eon of bloodshed, betrayal, and worst of all, the absence of what makes the world we live in so beautiful.

As much as I try to leave violence behind, I know it will always be there, lurking, unhidden. I understand the circumstances in which violence has yielded seemingly positive outcomes, but simple violence develops into a more horrific entity: vengeance.

For it's an infinite cycle that has no end. Its cure is without, but healing and love can mend for only a short while. The millennia past is not without peace, but war and violence will always be the sights and events that we remember. I wonder, Why is that?

Does it harken back to the times of old, when the weaker were trampled on by the strong? Is it in our nature to survive, and when pushed to the edge, we choose violence rather than love?

Self-affliction, destruction, anger, hate—we are all capable of producing. We are born this way, and there is no changing it. To learn to turn the other cheek is, *by god*, the hardest thing in the world to consider when it's so much easier to gouge out the eyes of our enemies.

The people who have betrayed us, misplaced our trust, destroyed what could've been. There is no alternate path we have chosen to take; violence will forever be what it is.

Humanity is violence, yes. Humanity is also a bounty of other admirable traits. We are not all good, nor all evil. The struggle is the villain to some, but I see it as our hopeful teacher.

I have learned that the cycle can be broken, but it takes choosing to heal rather than to harm. As easy as it is to strike back in ways we can't fathom, we were able to think about the destruction of another. I have seen that I'm feeding the monster inside of me. It will forever be a beast I fear but must love.

For what greater goal is there? To subside our hateful needs and subject ourselves to the love that we can produce just the same?

I love you, and you may not love me, but I will do my best to keep loving. In the name of violence, I attest…

Unbound, unrelenting, eternal *are words to describe it, but I will no longer yield to your call. Harbor my hate, harbor my shortsightedness, harbor my sins, for I choose to love and hope for the best than succumb to the broken cycle that is…*

Violence.

STROKE

It's a Metaphor

Your skin is tender. My hand grazes down your backside as I press in. The warmth, it's compelling. You bite, I moan. Stroke.

Lavender and vanilla blossom your hair as I pull on each blessed strand. The entanglement—I can feel it already. We press on. *Stroke.*

Your eyes, they stare. They stare gently, almost as if they have known me forever. Attraction with a gaze, and I'm compelled to pull closer. *Stroke.*

Music plays, but it's not what you're thinking. Natural, exuberant, and pure, a description of the angels choiring from the bond. *Stroke.*

Your lip pierces. You pierce me. Blood is drawn, a pact forged. Stroke.

Climax, it's coming. This time can't end. I don't want it to. I've been stricken down with an illness. I know the diagnosis, and there is no cure. Our skin grips as the music motions to our hips, and I hold on. I am not afraid, because I love this madness. *Stroke...*

An epilogue, the ending and a beginning. The first stroke to initiate a million more. Infinite possibilities all forged because of you. *Stroke.*

COFFEE

Bittersweet Kisses

Bitter and sweet, hot and cold.
I reach for your hand, and without hesitation, you grasp it.
Three words fall from my gaping maw: How are you?
We sip, and you talk, and most importantly, I listen.
You tell me that it has been hard ever since he left...
I know, and I'm sorry that he gave up on you.
He didn't know what he had.
The love that flowed from you with each passing moment must've overwhelmed him.
You lean, and I stay.
No, this isn't the answer.
Please don't label me as such.
I don't want to provide any more heartbreak, because I'm not ready.
I get up, and I order another. I look back and I ask, "Bitter or Sweet?"
You reply, "Sweet."
Ah, now we are getting somewhere.
I sit once again, and the mood has changed accordingly. *Evolution.*
We talk further, and you and I share a moment that I have but dreamed about.
The eternal sunshine of hope that envelopes between our fingers.
I'm not ready, and I don't think I will be anytime soon, I say.
You understand, and for the first time, you kiss me on the cheek.
You get up, and I stay.
Before you go, you grab the coffee.
As you walk out the door, you turn and wink.
I say, "This is a beautiful beginning, you know."
"I know, and I will be waiting when you want to start."

BETTER
Potential Is Worth More Than Gold

You know it, yet I'm afraid.
A potential to be...
Potential, I see it in you as well.
Are we afraid?
Can we become something better than both?
Salvation.

BLUE NEON

Nobody Knows

I remember this one time; it was just you and me.
We were…strolling—no, we were dancing.
Lights of neon were flaring, flashing, buzzing under our movements.
It was you, me, and the music.
Freedom, an expression of it at the least.
I saw you, free. It was wonderous, wild, out-of-control enjoyment.
It was then that I speculated that no one knew you in here.
You were by yourself, having the time of your life.
I sat in the corner, waiting.
You see, I was scheming.
I was plotting the perfect entrance to jump into the fray.
Then…
Oh, then you caught me.
For the first time you withdrew from your stronghold, and I…
I was defenseless.
You surged toward me like a bull to his matador.
I couldn't help but be entangled in your tussle.
I placed my arm forward, and before I knew it, I was basking in neon.
Forever lost on that plane that no one knew was created that day.

CREATION
Another Metaphor...Ugh

Molding.
Molding between my hands.
I stretch, I peel, I prong, I press, I roll.
So much is possible that I begin to question, What is the impossible?
I am fragile, but you help me bend.
You create me as I create you.
Together we become...we become a new creation of sorts.
Something, *and with pride I say this*, and nothing like us has ever graced itself on this plane.
Yet you were made for me, and me you.
As we peel away the layers, we dissect and stretch to places thought locked and keyed.
I press further, and at first the horror strikes.
Are we ready? You pull deeper. A profound and simple gesture washes the fear away.
We mold again, and for the last and first time, we mold together.
Feeling, we have created, you and me.
It was a mold that was unbreaking.
You and I and the creation unfolding between us, *magnificence*.

DREAM, FOR HUMANITY

You see, in the entirety of creation, there has been a dream. A dream that life will prosper.

A dream that under the intense pressure of the ever-finite abyss, against the interstellar odds of surviving in a universe set to its own self-destruct sequence, there has been a dream that we can achieve more.

I dream.

I dream that one day we may all prosper.

For some, they may have reached the most pleasurable form of prosperity, bless be. I dream that one day I will be a part of that all-too-foreign hope.

As foreign as the dream may seem, I find myself pondering. Pondering as to how we are given so much in the time we have, yet the time I have is substantially less than the cycle of creation.

Let me ask you this: If there was just one dream, just one dream in the entirety of human thought, what would it be?

It doesn't matter, *the answer anyways*. Though, I have a dream.

I have a dream that life will continue to thrive as long as there are people dreaming.

Life will prosper. After all, isn't that the dream?

A WOMAN
Named Desire

I see you. I see you sitting there, book in hand, reading intently. It's mesmerizing, and you glance up to catch me staring. I smile, and you smile back. Awkwardness subsides, and I get up from my seat. I approach, and she begins to move her belongings around; the coffee stays unmoved.

Aroma dances through the room, and the smell is captivating, but you...you are supremely so. The pull is magnetizing, and as I approach, your aura feeds the pull.

I approach, slightly hesitant, and I ask her if I may take a seat. She replies, "You may." I pull from the table, and I take a seat. It's warm, but no one was sitting here prior. How is that? "Did you do it?" She giggles, and I ask, "What are you reading?"

"Well, wouldn't you like to know..."

I smirk, and a laugh escapes from my mind, slipping with purpose.

I smile, and she smiles back. I reply, "Ah, so it's going to be like that..."

I reach down into my bag and pull; two can play this game.

I pull from my collection, and on the table the coffee boils. The tension rises, but it's blissful. The book makes its mark on the hallowed wood, and she comments, "Ah, Hemingway. You must appeal to the dark, then?"

"Darkness is not the absence of light, but it's the presence of pure thought. A canvas waiting to be...painted."

She nods. I sip...

You know, I think you might be lucky enough to discover my birthright.

I turn away and signal to the waiter; two fingers rise, and he knows...espresso. "Let me guess, Fitzgerald? No, wait, Kaur?"

"Well done. Now, put that book down and tell me…tell me what inspires you."

"Well, to be completely honest, and the answer may sound ridiculous, but it's…the desire to know your name."

Espresso places itself on the table. I nod. She sips. "Will I ever be that lucky, or must I inquire further" Perhaps.

We sip.

HONESTY

A Love Letter

I lay in a field. I don't know where, but I'm with you, my everything. I never imagined it would be like this, floating. I feel like I'm floating when I am near you, your grace, your essence, your truth; I simply adore. Magnetizing, you pull yourself toward me, and I you. We waver on the edge of the abyss, yet I hold your hand knowing you won't let go. See, that's the thing about honesty. I trust you. "Till death do us part" and such.

The breeze brushes the tall grass as we ponder the mysterious creations floating in the crystal sky. I glance to her, and she glances back. I begin to vocalize something poetic, and then lighting strikes. "I lied." It hasn't hit me. I continue my conversation. Her face looks at me as if I hadn't heard what she said, then my mind backtracks. Oh. Oh, oh god. How? When? Why?

It hurts. It hurts more than I could ever imagine, stabbing again, and again, and again. I'm bleeding now. My lifeline severed in a sentence. One thought protrudes the most through the pain, and I can't bear to accept it yet. I gave you everything, unconditional. A vow broken, and a history fractured. The end of an era. As her voice pierces what's left of me, I simply turn away. Muddled and mumbled, her pitch increases, and it drowns in the background no matter how hard she tries. Never again. Never…again.

I lay in a field. I don't know where, but I am no longer with you. A lifetime of honesty thrown away in seconds, yet it's as much my fault as yours. We walked away from each other too soon. That one thought that kept poking. Forgiveness. A stronger bond than honesty could ever forge. The memory reruns like a bad sitcom, and I look up to the same crystal sky with each creation passing by. I am okay. I breathe. A decision solidifies.

You hurt me. The type of hurt that takes a lifetime to heal from. But we were something. I cannot ignore that. The pull, the attraction, the chemistry—it's perfect. So in choosing this (which, let me tell you, the decision did not come easy), I ask you, Do you accept my ability to forgive? The answer paints her face before a word slips from her lips. I pull forward, and the attraction magnifies. A rekindling. As we draw closer, I ask her the one thing that will be the start to another arduous journey. I ask, "Be honest, did you ever stop loving me?" She waits, but the time passing is not hesitation. She wraps her hands in mine.

Her lips move…

"Honestly, how could I?"

Come Here
Dawnmarie Deshaies

ABOUT THE AUTHOR

Robert Deshaies II is a student, writer, poet, and lover of all literature. He collects comic books, graphic novels, and many poetry books. He has an obsession with early-twentieth-century writers that have thus influenced his life to pursue the writing works presented before you. Damn, Fitzgerald and Hemingway. He is booky, a lover of superheroes, the entire comic median (Batman, especially; why, he's awesome!). Robert is also an avid coffee drinker, some say in excess amounts. He is currently developing upcoming projects focusing on screenplays, a collection of short stories, a series of graphic novels, and of course, more poetry to sate his hopeless romantic soul.

CPSIA information can be obtained
at www.ICGtesting.com
Printed in the USA
FSHW011905241120
76243FS